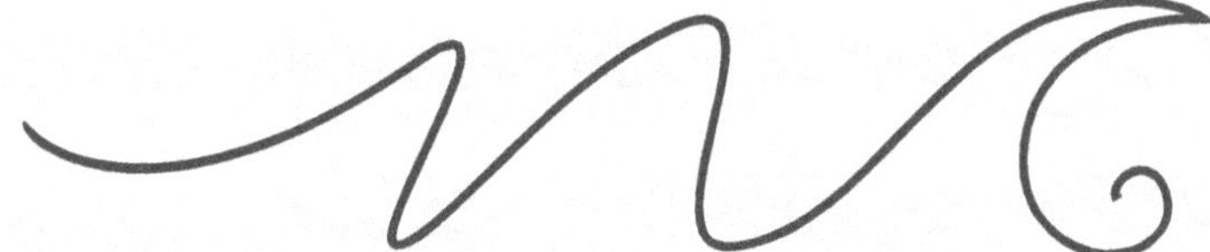

# the nature of grief

## A CREATIVE WORKBOOK FOR SEASONS OF HEALING

MELINDA LAUS

Published by The Nature of Grief, 2024
Portland, Oregon USA
thenatureofgrief.com



Edited by Jenna Thompson
Cover design and interior layout by Emily Coats

Photography by Michelle Humphrey (cover, 1, 14, 29, 48, 57), Emily Coats (vi, 2, 5, 8, 12, 14, 20, 24, 30, 46, 58, 64, 70, 78, 82, 87, 88, 92, 94, 97, 103, 106), Melinda Laus (33, 36, 61, 73), Daniel Kirsch (17), Josephine Bredehoft (34), Thomas Didgeman (42), Jay Mantri (62), Roland Steinmann (67), Neringa Olbutaite (68), Monika Leoni (81), Jessica Joh (100), Filippo Sarci (104)



The text of *Seasons for Healing Workbook* is set in Freight Sans Pro designed by Joshua Darden. Additional typefaces include Wild Nebraska designed by Larin Type Co.

ISBN-13: 979-8-2184276-3-4

*Dear Reader,*

I wrote this book for you in the hopes that you will not feel so alone in your grief. These pages are an offering of insights and practices I've discovered over the years — not only as a grief counselor but also as a fellow griever.

I have been learning from and living with grief since the unexpected death of my husband David in 2003. We were in our early 30s, happily married, completely in love with each other and our two little boys. Then, on an ordinary morning, I got a phone call from David's work. He had experienced a sudden cardiac event and his heart stopped.

Suddenly I was a widow. And a single parent.

Since David's death, I have been asked countless times how I "got through" it. While this is an understandable question, it has always felt impossible to answer. It took years to recognize the alchemy of elements that brought respite, connection, and understanding through my grief. I have taken notes along the way, hoping I might one day share what I have learned about grief and how I've experienced healing.

Being in nature and closely observing its beauty and wonder tops my list. Nature is spacious enough to hold our sorrow gracefully. It helps us make more room for loving and grieving what we've lost. This workbook invites you to bring your attention to the beauty and wonder of the natural world. It invites you to observe, reflect, and find connection in your grief.

*Melinda*

# HOW TO USE THIS BOOK

This workbook was designed as a companion through your seasons of healing after loss. It invites you to connect with different elements of nature as sources of metaphor and inspiration and as catalysts for your own healing process. The writing and photography prompts can be used as reflections or meditations. The blank spaces on the pages are invitations to write, draw, collage, press flowers or leaves, or create whatever feels good to express.

Grief is not a linear process with tidy beginnings and endings. Neither is this workbook. You are welcome to start on any page and visit any season or element that feels right for you on any given day. There is no "right" way to grieve and there is no "right" way to use this workbook.

Remember, you are not alone in your grief. We all need community on our journey. This book was created as a further guide and companion for The Seasons for Healing online community. You are welcome to join us at **thenatureofgrief.com**.

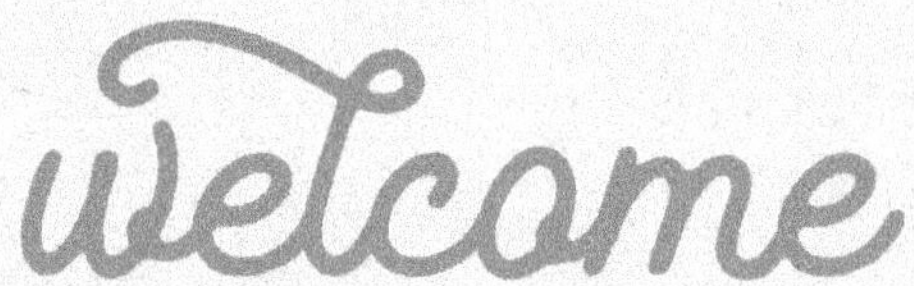

# welcome

In my early grief, I would pick up a new book about grief and feel a flutter of hope that somehow it would offer a cure for my sadness.

I experienced moments of agreement, recognition, or connection as I read these books, and they often helped me feel less alone. Yet disappointment always followed. Reading them was like seeing part of my face in a broken mirror: they didn't fully reflect my experience or cure my sorrow. They never "fixed it". I longed for a book that would help me feel completely seen and understood. While each writer shared their unique story, and while there were places where our experiences overlapped, no two experiences were exactly the same. No one was fully like me.

Grief has a way of making us feel separate from each other and the bigger world. It fractures us into a million shards of what we were before. Yet even though nothing fixes it, we can still find things that help. We can still find connection, support, and healing.

Over the past twenty years, I have discovered that the stillness of nature offers a respite from the intensity of grief. I've learned that grief is intrinsically part of love, and that befriending grief connects us to love more deeply than we knew was possible.

The following pages cannot cure your grief but they can offer a safe and comforting place to explore your path through it. As you turn the pages, I hope you feel a connection to me and all the other like-hearted grievers in this world. I hope you connect more deeply with your love for your beloved and for yourself.

# Contents

Winter

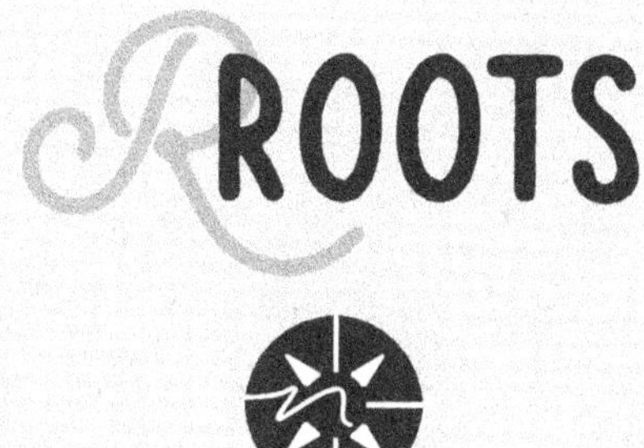

# ROOTS

The roots of any living being are a source of both strength and vulnerability. Roots anchor a plant to the earth, deliver nutrients from the soil, and send and receive messages, yet one powerful storm can rip the roots from the ground and leave them exposed and raw.

Humans are no different. Our roots are a paradoxical source of strength and vulnerability, and losing someone we love forces us to bear the paradox in ways we never imagined. Grief leaves us exposed. We become ungrounded and our vulnerable roots need protection.

Your habits, beliefs, and relationships are all part of your root system. In times of loss, this intricate web can be a source of courage and strength you never knew you had. Needing deep care and connection means you need support. It's a sign of strength to ask for support in moments of weakness. When you are weak and broken, asking for support offers the possibility of being seen, being known, and being loved just as you are.

**WRITING PROMPT**

What does being rooted feel like for you now? What did it feel like when your loved one was here?

When you are in nature this week, look for places where roots are exposed. If those roots could share their wisdom with you, what would they say?

Nourishment comes in many forms—physical, emotional, spiritual.
How are you grounding and nourishing yourself today?

What is threatening your grounded-ness?

**PHOTOGRAPHY PROMPT**

Find pictures of the roots you see in the world around you.
This might be the exposed roots of trees or the tiny roots of
the potted plant on your counter. Can you capture images
that tell the story of roots and grief in your life?

#  STORMS

A powerful storm can transform a landscape. Relentless rain becomes a flood; a crack of lightning can start a fire or topple a tree; wind can rip the shingles from rooftops. Storms can help us when we're grieving because they are an outward reflection of our inner turmoil. They connect us to the anguish of grief. Losing someone we love reminds us of our powerlessness against the arc of life in this world—an arc that includes death.

We can't bring our loved ones back from the other side. Somehow we have to integrate the anguish of loss into our ongoing life.

Your experience of anguish will transform your inner landscape just as a storm transforms the outer landscape. This transformation has the paradoxical capacity to create new shapes and possibilities even as it destroys what was there before. Storms of anguish are not here to destroy *you*. They're part of the dramatic transformation that grief brings to each of our lives.

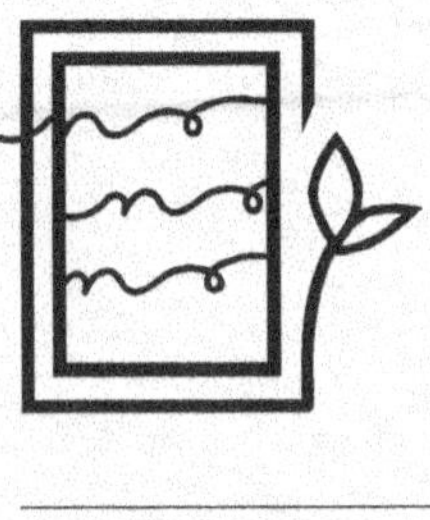

### WRITING PROMPT

Write about an experience of anguish in your grief. What helped you get through that moment?

What has surprised you the
most in your grief?

Tell the story of a storm you have lived through.
Describe any feelings of helplessness or
powerlessness against the force of nature.

### *PHOTOGRAPHY PROMPT*

Find pictures of storm clouds or the signs of past storms
in your environment. This could be an uprooted tree or
standing water after a heavy rain. Capture the anguish you
feel in your grief. What pictures tell the story of your sorrow?

We can't see the wind but we can feel its strength.
We see how it uproots trees and hurls waves against
the shore and moves anything that stands in its way.
This show of power is enviable when the rage of grief
surges inside us. We wish we could hurl waves or
uproot trees with our bare hands, but we're not the
wind. We don't have the wind's power. Feeling this
rage in our bodies without a clear path of release is
like punching underwater or swinging a paper sword.

What are we supposed to do when we feel this way?
Anger is a basic human emotion and yet we don't
have much guidance about how to feel and express it
without harming ourselves or others. To make things
even harder, we often judge our anger for being
irrational or unreasonable.

Your anger is not something you need to change or
fix. It's not a sign of failure. Anger connects you to
your sorrow that things aren't the way they should
be. Anger is a deep protest against circumstances you
didn't choose and that you don't want. It's not here to
drain you or leave you powerless. When things aren't
as they should be, anger is completely normal. Feeling
angry makes sense.

What happens if you approach anger as if you're in
a relationship with it? What if you let yourself find
safe, healthy ways to express its energy—whether
smashing plates or screaming in the car or throwing
yourself into a physically demanding activity—and let
yourself trust that even this is part of healing?

## WRITING PROMPT

What were you taught about anger when you were growing up? How were you encouraged to express it? How were you discouraged from expressing it?

WRITE ABOUT WHAT MAKES YOU ANGRY IN YOUR GRIEF.

Write about a favorite scene from a movie or book where a
character expresses their anger. What happens in the scene?
How did it make you feel? Was humor perhaps part of the scene?

## PHOTOGRAPHY PROMPT

Find pictures that capture the wind's movement—the way it moves the branches, rustles through tall grass, or ripples the surface of a lake or a puddle. Take self-portraits of yourself expressing anger. Notice how it feels in your body to make facial expressions of anger.

In the winter, empty fields look lifeless. It's hard to
imagine—especially under a dark winter sky —that
anything could grow there again. In many ways,
fallow fields are a tangible depiction of loss because
they give a physical shape to the hollowness and
hopelessness of sorrow.

The word *fallow* literally means "a period of time
characterized by inaction; unproductive," yet farmers
will tell you that fallow fields are regenerating nutrients
and actively resting to revitalize themselves. They
are in a constant state of communication with their
own chemistry and restoration. These are all deeply
productive activities. In this way, a fallow field invites
you to accept exactly what you need when you're
grieving: Space. Rest. Purposeful unproductivity.

A fallow field is a picture of paradox. It's actively
inactive. It's fruitfully barren. Its emptiness promises
fullness. In your grief and healing process, you have
permission to rest, replenish, and rebuild your
energy and nourishment. You have permission to
enter the flow of still *being* and active *doing*. Even
in our fallowness, even during seasons when we
feel hopeless, barren, and unproductive, a quiet
restoration may still be unfolding.

**WRITING PROMPT**

Write about your experience of rest in your grief. Explore the permission you do or don't give yourself to be purposely unproductive.

Write about the messages you have absorbed about rest. Did your family value rest or did they see it as lazy? How do those messages influence your ability to rest in your grief?

Write about a time you made the bed **OR** write about the place (real or imagined) where you rest.

_______________________________________________

_______________________________________________

_______________________________________________

_______________________________________________

_______________________________________________

_______________________________________________

_______________________________________________

_______________________________________________

_______________________________________________

_______________________________________________

### *PHOTOGRAPHY PROMPT*

Find pictures of fallow fields. This might be an actual farm field, a vacant lot, or any open space where the ground is untended. Take in the emptiness of these spaces. Notice the quality and color of the soil and how the shape of the ground is revealed.

# SELF PORTRAIT

Even when you are grieving, your life is still happening. You are alive. You are a part of nature. Create an image that represents you in this moment of your healing. This could be a photo, a picture from nature, a collage, or a drawing.

# THE NATURE OF YOUR GRIEF
## *in winter*

Tender Days & Anniversaries

_________________________________________

_________________________________________

_________________________________________

_________________________________________

_________________________________________

_________________________________________

_________________________________________

_________________________________________

_________________________________________

_________________________________________

Moods & Other Observations

_________________________________________

_________________________________________

_________________________________________

_________________________________________

_________________________________________

_________________________________________

_________________________________________

_________________________________________

_________________________________________

_________________________________________

Places in nature that offered
comfort & respite

- 
- 
- 
- 
- 

Things that brought
peace & comfort

- 
- 
- 
- 
- 

Spring

In the Pacific Northwest, moss is the living evidence of a rain-soaked landscape. In the forest, bright clumps of juniper haircap moss cling to tree trunks. Cat-tail moss trails from branches. Feathery beaked moss crowns the stumps of Douglas Firs and carpets the forest floor. Moss makes a home on bits of bark and fallen branches. It finds a way to grow even when there's too much water and not enough sunlight. In conditions that seem inhospitable, moss hangs on. It finds a way to thrive.

Poet Kahlil Gibran writes, "We are the seeds of the tenacious plant, and it is in our ripeness and our fullness of heart that we are given to the wind and are scattered." One definition of tenacious is "persisting in existence". In our own way, aren't we like moss in our grief? Something inside us hangs on. Our hearts keep beating, our lungs keep inhaling and exhaling, and our minds keep grappling and trying to understand. We reflect a courageous determination to survive—even when we don't feel strong or courageous.

Perhaps without intending it, you are living out a tenacious chapter in your life. You are persisting in your own existence even with the pain and sorrow you feel through grief.

**WRITING PROMPT**

Grieving people are often praised for 'being strong'. Write about your reaction to being called strong through your grief. Where do you struggle to feel capable in your life?

Write your own definitions of the words *resilient*, *tenacious*, and *strong*. Notice how those words feel different. Notice how and where these different feelings live within your body.

## COLLAGE

Create a collage that represents your courage in your grief.
This could be a calendar page with the days you showed up and
got things done. It could be images of where your loved one
is buried or where you scattered their ashes. Gather imagery,
quotes, colors, or words that reflect your persistance.

### PHOTOGRAPHY PROMPT

Photograph the moss in your environment. It might be growing between sidewalk cracks or on the trunks and branches of trees. If your camera allows, zoom in to capture the textures, patterns, and shapes of the moss.

In much of the northern hemisphere, spring might
as well be called the season of mud. Snowmelt and
heavy rain saturate the ground and turn everything
into a muddy, inescapable mess. Noticing all this
mud can give us insight into the different kinds of
pain we experience as humans, especially through
our grief.

One kind of pain is 'clean pain'. Clean pain is
the initial wound that causes us to feel grief,
loss, sorrow, or suffering. Clean pain is directly
connected to the death of your loved one; it is your
authentic experience of losing them.

But 'dirty pain' is different. Dirty pain is the added
suffering we put on ourselves—like survivor guilt,
or feeling like we aren't recovering fast enough, or
replaying the past days and weeks of our loved one's
life and feeling tortured by the fear that we could
have done more to love them or save them. Dirty
pain muddies the water around our clean pain. It adds
more suffering to the pain we are already experiencing.
It makes the burden of grief even heavier.

When we notice that we're overthinking and
blaming ourselves, we can remember that death is
bigger than any of us. We do not have control over
it. In those moments when the muddiness of dirty
pain is making it hard to see clearly, we can extend
more compassion to ourselves. Dirty pain doesn't
tell us the truth about our loss; it is a signal that we
need more self-compassion.

# MUD

**WRITING PROMPT**

What is the clean pain—the initial wound—of your grief? Write about the difference between the clean pain and the dirty pain that you feel.

Write a letter to yourself where you express compassion and admiration for the way you're enduring the pain of loss. Use the page as a place to practice talking to yourself with compassion.

# Write about a messy time in your relationship with your loved one.

How was this messiness resolved? Do you wish there had been a different resolution? If so, let yourself rewrite the ending.

Find pictures of mud in your environment. Go exploring for mud puddles or muddy patches of ground. Notice the patterns in the mud. Notice the footprints or animal tracks. Find pictures that tell the story of muddiness in grief. Capture images to represent the clean and dirty pain you are experiencing.

Water is a source of cleansing and renewal, and spring rain has a particular gentleness, as if it's bathing the earth with kindness. This spring, notice how water moves and gathers in the landscape around you. Notice the fresh rainfall and snowmelt, the trickling rivulets and rising creeks, the puddles and marshy fields. Notice the way rain slides down a window or pools under a downspout.

In Chinese medicine, water connects us to the flow of our energy. Water is considered "yin" energy, which is gentle and healing. Yin energy dissolves anxiety and helps us live in a more restful flow. One way to show kindness to yourself is by taking time to be near water. This can be as simple as watching the rain. As you watch, feel how your breath moves. Feel the flow as you slowly inhale and exhale. Notice any sensations of ease, lightness, or calm. Take the time to let your body absorb these sensations.

So much has changed for you. You are grieving the one you love. You are grieving the future you had envisioned. You are grieving the changes in relationships that have become disappointing or hurtful. Remember that the feelings of ease, lightness, or calm that emerge when you watch the rain—or anytime you're near water—are available in other ways, too. You can let go of relationships that are heavy; you can surround yourself with people who bring the same gentle kindness as the rain.

## WRITING PROMPT

Write about the relationships that bring comfort, connection, and a sense of safety. Write about the relationships where you feel less comfortable sharing about your struggles and sadness. Notice any themes that emerge in your relationships.

Write about a memorable
experience of the rain.

Rain has a cleansing quality, like the tears we shed when we are grieving. Write about your experience with your tears through your grief. Where and when are you most able to cry? What elements in nature or your environment help you feel safe enough to release your sorrow?

_______________________________________________

_______________________________________________

_______________________________________________

_______________________________________________

_______________________________________________

_______________________________________________

_______________________________________________

_______________________________________________

_______________________________________________

_______________________________________________

_______________________________________________

### PHOTOGRAPHY PROMPT

Take pictures that capture the mood and movement of the rain. This might be on an actual rainy day or it might just be the water on your windshield in the carwash. Capture any image that represents the kindness you have received in your grief. Maybe kindness arrived via a beautiful sunset or a quiet rainy morning. Maybe it came via cards, letters, or food from people who care about you. Find any image that tells the story of kindness after loss.

Do you remember what it was like in elementary school when you learned about monarch butterflies for the first time? Their journeys seemed too impossible to be real: an egg becomes a caterpillar, a caterpillar becomes a chrysalis, and a chrysalis becomes a brilliant red-and-gold monarch that migrates 3,000 miles—a feat of stamina, survival, and adaptation.

Even then, we were learning that change is constant. We were learning that transformation means that something changes shape. We were learning that these transformations happen not just to butterflies, but also to us.

The fact that change is constant might be obvious, but less obvious is that transformation and loss go together. Transformation is an ongoing pattern of beginnings and endings. Entering a new phase means leaving something behind.

When we're grieving, we might long for earlier versions of ourselves.

# BUTTERFLIES

We might miss who we used to be. We might want to skip ahead to a different part of the process or wonder who we will become. All these longings are part of our ongoing journey.

Our culture tends to focus on what it sees as the "final result" of transformation, the part of the process where beautiful wings unfurl. We don't usually celebrate the nurturing and gathering of the caterpillar as she eats every leaf in her path or her dark months in the chrysalis. Yet the gorging and growing—followed by waiting—are also worth celebrating. Every stage of your transformation, every pang of longing, is worth honoring.

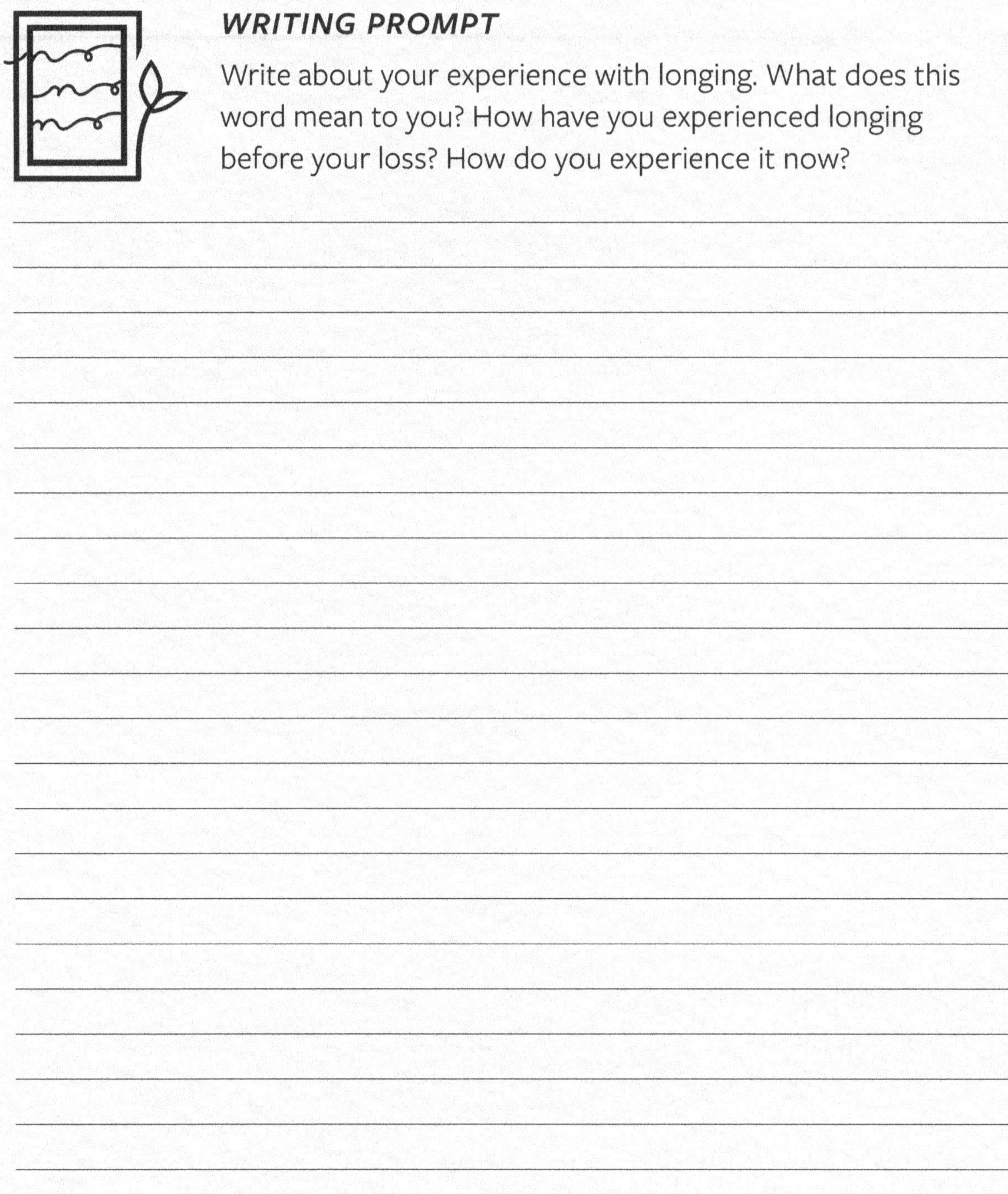

## WRITING PROMPT

Write about your experience with longing. What does this word mean to you? How have you experienced longing before your loss? How do you experience it now?

## How do you experience transformation in your life?

Are you a seeker and a studier who needs books
and learning in order to embrace change?
Are you a protestor who pushes against change?
Are you a weeper who acknowledges change with
tears and releases the 'what was' to make room for
the 'what shall be'?

Write about your connection to butterflies.
How do you react when you see them?

What do they represent to you?

How has your grief transformed?

How have you been transformed by your grief?

### *PHOTOGRAPHY PROMPT*

If you are lucky enough to capture a photograph of butterflies, please do! If they prove elusive, then take or find pictures of anything that represents transformation: a tight rosebud next to a fully bloomed rose, a leaf unfurling or changing color, a bright yellow dandelion next a white puff of dandelion seeds. Take pictures of anything in the landscape that represents change.

## SELF PORTRAIT

Even when you are grieving, your life is still happening. You are alive. You are a part of nature. Create an image that represents you in this moment of your healing. This could be a photo, a picture from nature, a collage, or a drawing.

# THE NATURE OF YOUR GRIEF
## *in spring*

Tender Days & Anniversaries

_______________________________

_______________________________

_______________________________

_______________________________

_______________________________

_______________________________

_______________________________

_______________________________

_______________________________

_______________________________

Moods & Other Observations

_______________________________

_______________________________

_______________________________

_______________________________

_______________________________

_______________________________

_______________________________

_______________________________

_______________________________

_______________________________

Places in nature that offered
comfort & respite

- 
- 
- 
- 
- 

Things that brought
peace & comfort

- 
- 
- 
- 
- 

Summer

Imagine stepping into a grove of tall trees on a hot summer afternoon. The shade cools your skin and protects you from the sharp sunlight; the air moves gently through the leaves. In that moment, if you close your eyes and listen, it's as if the trees are your ancestors—encircling you, shielding you. They create a container of coolness to protect you from the overwhelm of too much exposure.

The respite of a shady grove teaches us how to take care of ourselves when we are overwhelmed. Feeling overwhelmed in grief is normal. We often respond to overwhelm by working harder, making more lists, trying to focus our thoughts, and punishing ourselves with even more demands—as if checking things off a list will make the overwhelm go away. In reality, we're more likely to experience relief by ignoring our lists and resting in a protected place.

What if feeling overwhelmed is a signal that you need respite? What if overwhelm is not here to punish you or push you, but rather to invite you to take refuge in a shady, protected circle where the only sound is rustling leaves?

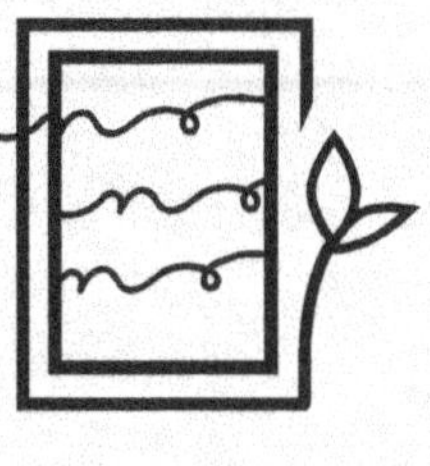

## WRITING PROMPT

Write about a time you felt overwhelmed this week. How did you get through it? What caused the feelings of overwhelm? Was it unwashed dishes in the sink, a pile of unpaid bills, or a pet that left a mess on the floor?

WHEN I FEEL OVERWHELMED, THE SENSATIONS IN MY BODY FEEL LIKE

WHEN I FEEL OVERWHELMED, MY THOUGHTS SOUND LIKE

WHEN I FEEL OVERWHELMED, I WORRY ABOUT

WHEN I FEEL OVERWHELMED, I WISH SOMEONE WOULD

WHEN I FEEL OVERWHELMED, I WISH SOMEONE WOULD TELL ME

THE NEXT TIME I FEEL OVERWHELMED I HOPE I

Write about one of the best nights
of sleep you've ever had.

Find a shady spot in a park or near a grove of trees or tall bushes. Notice how you feel as you focus on the changing light. Find or take a picture that represents the feeling of being overwhelmed. Find or take a picture that represents respite from overwhelm.

In grief, many of us are anxious about how to honor our loved one after they have died. It's easy to feel overwhelmed—by our grief, by the desire to honor their life in a tangible way, and by the feeling that we're not doing enough. The pressure of insufficiency mounts as days and weeks and years pass, seemingly pulling us farther away from their lifetime.

We do not want our beloved's life to be forgotten. The drive to remember them, to keep them somehow present, is linked to our love for them.

This drive can also be a healing expression of our grief. It's the mourning part of our process. Grief is the internal feelings we experience after loss and mourning is the outward expression of those feelings. When we mourn, we are offering ourselves more healing. Every act of mourning can also be seen as a way to honor our loved ones. Some gestures are bigger and more visible: memorial runs, fundraisers, scholarships, plaques or statues in significant places. Yet we also

# PEBBLES, PINECONES, & SHELLS

need quieter rituals. It could be as simple as lighting a candle or creating a sacred space in your home. It could be gathering small gifts from the natural world—pebbles, pinecones, bits of moss, leaves, shells—and arranging them in a way that feels beautiful. Every hug you give, every song you sing, every deep breath of remembering is a way to honor your beloved. The way you mourn is enough. You are enough.

Write about the traditions and rituals you were raised with. How were you taught to honor your loved ones after they died?

How do you dream of publicly honoring your loved one's life?

How do you want to mourn?

Write about a ceremony you've witnessed that has always stayed with you.

Find a photo that captures any ritual, ceremony, or practice where you mourn your loved one. Photograph anything you might have created as an act of mourning. This might be a nature mandala, living sculpture, or other arrangement. Find or photograph pinecones, pebbles or shells in your landscape.

The Pacific Northwest coastline is rocky and rugged, with strong currents and choppy surf. Some waves are so unpredictable that they have a name: "Sneaker Waves". They come out of nowhere, sweeping high onto the beach with enough force to knock you off your feet and pull you out to sea.

# WAVES

We often hear that the emotions of grief come in waves. Emotions build, crest, retreat, then build again. In early grief we might be thrown off by their ebb and flow, or by a sudden "sneaker wave" that drags us down. Or our early grief might be marked by numbness and shock that has to wear thin before we feel the waves.

In our culture, we often try to control our emotions, yet the waves of grief are connected to your love for the one you've lost. Rather than trying to control the waves of grief, we can learn to trust their rhythm. We can learn to swim with the current rather than fight it.

Poet Rainer Maria Rilke wrote, "Let everything happen to you: beauty and terror. Just keep going. No feeling is final." Feelings aren't permanent, just like waves aren't permanent. Grief is full of flow. In and out. Crest and fall. Rise and recede. Holding on and letting go.

The waves of grief will eventually slow down. There will be more space between sets. There will be a time when the tenderness of longing for your loved one will not pull you under.

**WRITING PROMPT**

Write about your waves of grief. Is there a particular day—or time of day—that is hardest for you? Do your waves have a pattern or are they all sneaker waves?

How do you react to Rilke's words that "no feeling is final"?

Write about an experience you've had with waves in nature.

___________________________________________________________

___________________________________________________________

___________________________________________________________

___________________________________________________________

___________________________________________________________

___________________________________________________________

___________________________________________________________

___________________________________________________________

___________________________________________________________

___________________________________________________________

___________________________________________________________

### PHOTOGRAPHY PROMPT

If you can, visit the beach, a nearby lake, or anywhere you can see waves on water. Notice their rise and fall. Capture an image that represents where and how you're experiencing waves of grief.

# Waves of Grief

MY LAST GIANT GRIEF WAVE HAPPENED ON THIS DAY _______________________

THIS IS WHAT I DID TO RIDE THE WAVE _______________________
_______________________________________________________________
_______________________________________________________________
_______________________________________________________________

THE RIPPLES OF GRIEF LOOK LIKE _______________________________
_______________________________________________________________
_______________________________________________________________
_______________________________________________________________

I FEEL THE MEDIUM-SIZED GRIEF WAVES WHEN _______________________________

______________________________________________________________________

______________________________________________________________________

SMALLER GRIEF WAVES HAPPEN WHEN _______________________________________

______________________________________________________________________

______________________________________________________________________

Life is full of experiences that are inextricably linked, where opening to one kind of experience means simultaneously opening to another. Just as we cannot experience grief unless we have opened ourselves to love, we cannot experience loss without the simultaneous invitation to a deeper sense of wonder. In grief, this invitation to wonder comes via our experience of beauty. The combination of beauty and wonder creates a balm for our aching hearts.

While a sense of wonder occasionally arises unbidden—during moments when we are fully present to our senses and the world around us— we can also cultivate it. Cultivating wonder takes patience and gentleness, like approaching a butterfly.

No matter the season, beauty is woven into the natural world around you. It can be as simple as a potted ficus tree or as breathtaking as the alpine glow of a mountain peak at sunset. When we train our eyes and hearts to notice beauty, we open ourselves to wonder. Start with any flower— in your garden, in the neighborhood, or even at the store. Notice the shape and texture of the petals, the intensity of color, the scent. Then notice what else captures your attention. Paintings, light on dusty window sills, dewy spider webs reflecting tiny rainbows, the perfect dish of pasta, a stranger's gentle smile. Let beauty and wonder refresh your heart, no matter what form they happen to take.

Even as you are being transformed by loss, beauty is here to comfort you.

**WRITING PROMPT**

Write about how you are experiencing beauty through your loss. Is everything gray and foggy? Are colors especially bright and comforting?

In the book *Wild*, author Cheryl Strayed shared her mother's encouragement to "Put yourself in the way of beauty."

Write your response to these words. How can you put yourself in the way of beauty each day?

What is the relationship between wonder and grief in this
moment of your healing? Write about any experiences of wonder
that are giving you comfort or helping you find meaning.

## PHOTOGRAPHY PROMPT

Go outside and photograph anything that you find
beautiful—dahlias or roses or layers of clouds moving
across the sky. Find images that bring a sense of wonder.

## SELF PORTRAIT

Even when you are grieving, your life is still happening. You are alive. You are a part of nature. Create an image that represents you in this moment of your healing. This could be a photo, a picture from nature, a collage, or a drawing.

# THE NATURE OF YOUR GRIEF
## *in summer*

Tender Days & Anniversaries

_______________________

_______________________

_______________________

_______________________

_______________________

_______________________

_______________________

_______________________

_______________________

_______________________

Moods & Other Observations

_______________________

_______________________

_______________________

_______________________

_______________________

_______________________

_______________________

_______________________

_______________________

_______________________

Places in nature that offered
comfort & respite

- 
- 
- 
- 
- 

Things that brought
peace & comfort

- 
- 
- 
- 
- 

Autumn

We hear a lot of messages about "letting go" after loss. Comments like "you need to let go" or "you're going to have to let go eventually" imply that letting go is the only way to move forward. Yet grief looks different for everyone. In the fall, two trees might be standing right next to each other and yet one of them holds its red and gold leaves long after the other is down to bare branches. Leaves have their own timelines for letting go. Your experience of letting go will follow its own timeline, too. It doesn't have to make sense to others.

Of course, you don't have to let go at all. You are allowed to hold on. This doesn't have to make sense to others, either.

If and when the time comes, letting go can be as simple as finding yourself laughing at a funny movie or noticing the muscles in your neck loosen in a hot shower. Letting go could mean waking up with tears in your eyes and getting dressed anyway. It could mean releasing your dreams of what the future was supposed to look like and allowing new dreams to form instead.

Letting go sounds simple but it's delicate and often painful. It's about learning to trust yourself. It takes time and practice. No one will let go the way you do.

Just as trees have their own timelines for releasing their leaves, trust yourself and your own process. Trees don't chastise one another for their particular ways of letting go. They simply are. They simply do. You get to as well.

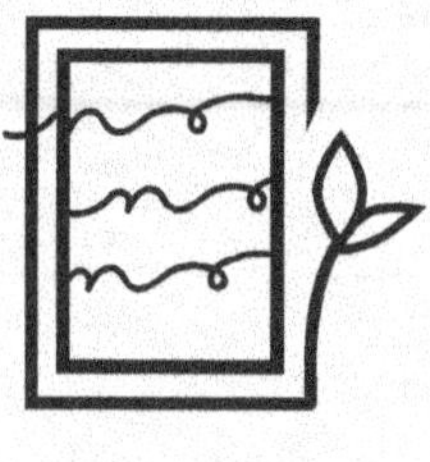

**WRITING PROMPT**

What does 'letting go' mean to you in your life? Explore your experiences of going through change. Do you welcome change or is it hard and full of contradictory emotions?

Write about what it means to give yourself
permission to let go—or to hang on—in your grief.

Write about a memorable fall day from your past.

Use your five senses to
describe how the day felt,
looked, tasted, sounded,
and smelled.

## PHOTOGRAPHY PROMPT

Take pictures of leaves that catch your eye this week. Notice
the leaves on the ground as well as those still on the branches.
Consider their various phases of changing colors and letting go.

When you're grieving, your brain is working hard: it's trying to process a devastating loss, trying to acclimate to a new life you never wanted, trying to solve the problem of death. All this energy and overthinking turns simple tasks into overwhelming challenges. The foggy condensation in your brain makes it impossible to follow a train of thought or make a decision. Finishing a task is ridiculously difficult. *Why did I walk into this room? Why did I only unload half the dishwasher? Why is everything for dinner on the counter but I cannot bring myself to get started?*

Brain fog, also known as "grief brain" is real. It muffles the energy you need to do everyday things. In a heavy fog, you can't be sure of what you're looking at and it's hard to judge distances. Brain fog functions the same way. Even familiar landscapes become strange and confusing. Your experiences are characterized by uncertainty and lack of clarity. You strain to make sense of things.

Yet brain fog is temporary. You haven't lost your ability to think. Your faculties will return. In the meantime, proceed as slowly as if you were driving in the fog. The swirl of confusion blurring the path is part of healing. Allow your muffled thoughts to burn through the fog and emerge in their own time. It is okay to slow down and orient yourself by focusing only on your next step

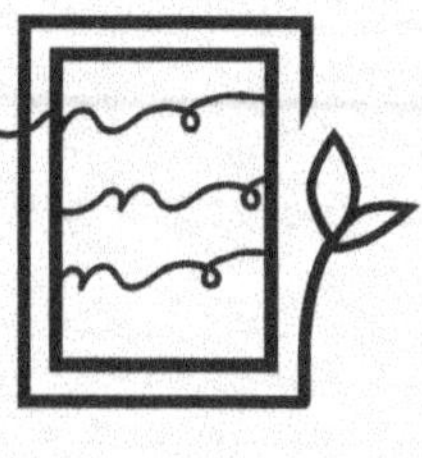



**WRITING PROMPT**

Write about your greatest fear with grief brain. Do you worry you will never be productive again or that your mind will always feel heavy and unclear?

## Where do you experience grief brain or foggy thinking the most right now?

Is it when you're at work? In a conversation?
Cooking a meal? Where is it hardest to concentrate?

How is your experience of grief similar to driving in the fog at night?

### PHOTOGRAPHY PROMPT

Take pictures that capture your experience of fogginess this week. It might be literal fog hanging in the trees or mist through a window. It might be another representation of what "grief brain" looks like—maybe a messy desk or piles of laundry or stacks of unopened mail. Collect images as if you are creating a documentary about grief to help others understand your experience.

# SUNFLOWERS

At this time of year, sunflowers are in full glory. Their skinny stalks and heavy golden blooms reflect the transition from summer to fall— sunny even as they signal the end of the bright season. Everywhere we look, the natural world reminds us that summer is slipping away. Hot days shift to cooler nights, leaves turn colors, bales of hay dot the fields, gardens are bountiful even as they show their fatigue. The growing season has come full circle, like the circle of each sunflower blossom.

This seasonal shift is heavy with longing—'a strong desire especially for something unattainable'. Many grievers experience a sharp rise in their longing at this time of year. It's like a wound that never heals. We're moving forward even as we long for what we've lost; we savor our memories even as we long for our loved one to still be here. We know this is impossible and yet we still long for what was and what might have been.

The feeling of longing hurts. It also—strangely, unexpectedly— offers a kind of wholeness. When we allow ourselves to connect with our longing, we encounter the bittersweet paradox of knowing our sorrow and remembering the beauty of our past. It is both bitter and sweet to let yourself remember. It's bitter and sweet to let yourself imagine the what-ifs. You are healing and hurting at the same time. Just as sunflowers hold both summer and fall, the experience of longing holds both loss and love.

**Write about bittersweetness. Where are you experiencing bitterness? Where are you experiencing sweetness? Is there a connection between them?**

*What does the transition from summer
to fall feel like for you?*

Sunflowers are heliotropes, which means they follow the sun.

Write about following the sun and what this means in your life.

### PHOTOGRAPHY PROMPT

Find sunflowers this week. Notice the patterns and intricacies of their stalks and blooms. If possible, visit a farm or garden and take in a full field of sunflowers.

# STARS

In each of our lives, there will be some people who simply can't cope with our pain. They might mean well, but their inability to be present to you (without trying to "make things better" or otherwise "encourage" you) means they should not have too much access to you. They might have the best of intentions and yet their impact is still damaging.

When you identify who these people are, you can honor yourself by creating new boundaries. This means there might be certain people you only see for 20 minutes at a time a few times a year. It might mean you avoid situations where there will be small talk. It might mean you say no to invitations.

Yet there are also people who will not flinch at your suffering and who will help you feel secure enough and safe enough to be honest about your experiences. They will validate your feelings. In the darkness of grief, these people are glimmers of light. They are like stars whose brightness reaches you even across a great distance. When grief completely transforms the maps of your relationships, and when you have to redraw your boundaries, these people are steady points of light that will help you find your way. They will help you find a community of healing that welcomes you as your are.

Who are the helpful stars that you can rely on in your grief?
What particular traits or support do they bring to you?

# Write about the things that do not help you in your grief.

What are the statements or platitudes that irritate or upset you?

WRITE ABOUT A MEMORABLE STARRY NIGHT YOU HAVE EXPERIENCED.

### PHOTOGRAPHY PROMPT

Take a portrait photo of the 'helpful stars' in your life. Ask them if you can take their picture to remember their support during this part of your healing.

# SELF PORTRAIT

Even when you are grieving, your life is still happening. You are alive. You are a part of nature. Create an image that represents you in this moment of your healing. This could be a photo, a picture from nature, a collage, or a drawing.

# THE NATURE OF YOUR GRIEF
## *in autumn*

Tender Days & Anniversaries

Moods & Other Observations

Places in nature that offered
comfort & respite

- 
- 
- 
- 
- 

Things that brought
peace & comfort

- 
- 
- 
- 
- 

# Acknowledgements

This book would not have been born without the expert care and support of Jenna Thompson. As my writing coach, editor, spiritual advisor and beloved confidante, Jenna has helped me in countless ways to bring this book to life. Her magical editorial skills, combined with her intuitive ability to nurture my creative spark, has brought this book into your hands. Thank you Jenna— I am forever grateful for you!

The beauty, design and structure of this book would not be possible without Emily Coats. Emily has been my creative co-conspirator, helping me to bring *The Nature of Grief* into being. Thank you Emily— for your vision, brilliance, wisdom and compassion. Your generous, wise heart is woven into every page of this book.

Thank you to my beloved first readers—

To Kim Johnson, who has always been my safe place to dream, to be creative, and to share my wild heart.

To Jennifer Nunes, who was one of my first young-widowed friends who generously read and supported this creative process with her wise and beautiful heart.

To Meg Eifrig, who is a fellow beloved griever, counselor and seeker of beauty. Thank you for being my trusted advisor and wise counsel on all the things.

To Lauren Selfridge, who held the vision and dream of this book with me. Your encouragement and ability to mirror my deepest feelings, dreams and hopes has kept me inspired and in love with this project.

To Barb Suarez, Jeffrey Davis, Marisa Goudy, Michaelene Ruhl and Jane Lee Rankin for being my creative inspiration and supportive pack. Your encouragement has made all the difference!

To my beloved family, Baba, Gaga, Brendan, Jonathan and Lauren— thank you for always believing in me. I love you more than words.

To David, for a lifetime of love.